DANIEL LAMBERT
A Life in Five Sittings

DANIEL LAMBERT
A Life in Five Sittings

Compiled and Edited by
MARK BLASDALE
2019

First Published Worldwide 2019

INTRODUCTION © Mark Blasdale 2019
All rights reserved. No part of this Introduction may be reproduced or transmitted in any form or by any means, electronic or mechanical, including photocopying, recording, or any information storage and retrieval system, without prior permission in writing by the copyright holder. The right of Mark Blasdale to be identified as the author of this work (Introduction) has been asserted by him in accordance with the Copyright, Designs and Patents Act 1988.

With the explicit exception of the Introduction, all other inclusions contained within this collection are in the Public Domain and are freely available, all being published prior to 1923. No right to copyright, ownership or title is claimed, implied or asserted for the following works:

THE ECCENTRIC MIRROR - 1806
THE ENGLISH ANNUAL - 1838
MUSIC AND FRIENDS: Or, Pleasant Recollections of a Dilettante - 1838
A GREAT IDEA (Household Words) - 1852
FAT PEOPLE (All the Year Round) - 1864

ISBN: 9781687712219

All Fonts used in this publication are designated *free fonts* by 1001fonts.com, fontspace.com, and premiumfonts.com

Cover image and Frontispiece: The Late Daniel Lambert Esq. Drawn from the Life. From: THE ECCENTRIC MIRROR 1806 - Public Domain.

www.markblasdale.com

This small volume is humbly and affectionately dedicated to the subject of its content,

Mr. Daniel Lambert.

"Lambert must not be suffered to sink into oblivion…"

- from *The English Annual*
By Omega
1838

CONTENTS

Introduction	Page 11
The Eccentric Mirror	Page 19
The English Annual	Page 52
Music and Friends	Page 79
A Great Idea (*extract*)	Page 85
Fat People (*extract*)	Page 88

"The Prince Regent was proud of his legs, and so was
Daniel Lambert, who was also a fat man;
he was proud of his legs."

- from *The Life and Adventures of Nicholas Nickleby*
by Charles Dickens
1839

INTRODUCTION

"*Lambert must not be suffered to sink into oblivion...*" So proclaimed the wit and author, Omega, in 'The English Annual' from 1838. Indeed, such was the popularity and celebrity of Leicester's *Great Pumpkin* during the 1800's that he was frequently in print. No less a personage than Charles Dickens was bent on keeping Lambert's memory before the public, casting Daniel as the anchor (so to speak) in two essays that appeared in his publications Household Words and All the Year Round, as well as calling upon Lambert's legs to make a brief appearance in his *'The Life and Adventures of Nicholas Nickleby.'*

As a child, I distinctly remember many visits to my native city's Newark House museum to gaze in wonder and astonishment at the bizarre collection of relics that were once the personal property of this great 'prodigy in nature'. Among these treasures was an armchair - a vast forest of mahogany almost three feet wide; a gnarled and twisted walking stick measuring some thirty-seven and a half inches in length, and his waistcoat and breeches, each memorably gargantuan in size. As schoolchildren, we would see how many could fit between the armrests of Daniel's chair; easily five, often more at a squeeze. Back on the familiar proving ground of the school yard, the time-honoured insult, *"You're a Danny Lambert"* would be hurled at any plump child, or contradictorily, at lean children too.

But the vast majority of my visits to Leicester's network of then-flourishing museums were conducted under the stewardship of a close neighbour and family friend. *'Aunt Connie'* (as we local children called her) was as passionate about literature and history as she was devoted to her two monstrously corpulent cats, Pickles and Podge. Biographical detail being somewhat sketchy, I will merely state that she was my academic cicerone; delighting in taking my brother and I on many expeditions into Leicester and detailing with unquestioned authority, tales of ghosts, hangings, and murders, as well as more highbrow pursuits in the then numerous museums of my home city. Her passion for local history was infectious and her love of Daniel Lambert doubly so. World history, literature and a general love of knowledge were unquestionably her legacy, and I owe her a lasting debt of gratitude.

Over the years, as life began to form and mould me, Daniel Lambert became part of faded memory; a *relic* of my childhood. By some strange coincidence, this also seemed to coincide with a sense of Lambert-related amnesia from the council too. For a city that would readily host a Roman-style *Triumph* to honour one of our occasionally successful sports teams, there always seemed a reluctance (to me at least) to do honour to the memory of our greatest son. Whether this was because having such abundant corpulency associated with the city was considered undesirable, only those who held office during those years can say. What is true, is that the city and county have never made *enough* of Lambert and his once universal celebrity.

I reacquainted myself with Daniel's story when I began to take my own writing more seriously. It alarmed me that, during the intervening years, nothing of his story had changed (and what there was seemed to be nothing more than rehashes of previous works). Academic enquiry seemed to somehow pass him by; of scholarly investigation -

nothing. All the sources for new retellings kept pointing back to the same handful of documents.

As I recall, the most widely available book on the subject when I was a child was published on behalf of the Museums and Art Gallery department of the local council. This, however, was a most unsatisfactory volume (if eighteen pages with minimal content could shoulder such an appellation), but with precious little else to feast upon, this 'pamphlet' became our staple diet on all matters Lambert-related.

The author of that particular book intriguingly mentioned as the main source of his micro-biography, a pamphlet printed at the time of Lambert's death, in 1809, entitled: 'THE LIFE OF THAT WONDERFUL AND EXTRAORDINARY HEAVY MAN, THE LATE DANIEL LAMBERT, FROM HIS BIRTH TO THE MOMENT OF HIS DISSOLUTION, WITH AN ACCOUNT OF MEN NOTED FOR THEIR CORPULENCY AND OTHER INTERESTING MATTER.' Tracking down a copy proved, as the reader might expect, somewhat difficult. However, and notwithstanding its catchy title, this, upon eventual reading, proved to be little more than a shameless pirating of an earlier biography featured prominently in 'THE ECCENTRIC MIRROR' and dated 1806.

I set about collecting further works in first edition format in order that I could feast upon the *original* rather than suffer them in regurgitated format. And now, having accumulated these antiquarian treasures, and sated my own appetite on their content, I thought it only correct and proper (as they are difficult to source and often price prohibitive) to lay them before the casual Lambert enthusiast to also enjoy in unmolested form.

Interestingly, THE LIFE OF THAT WONDERFUL AND EXTRAORDINARY HEAVY MAN, THE LATE DANIEL LAMBERT etc. etc. has, in recent years, attained a status amongst *some* Lambert biographers as the 'go to' source, something that is wholly undeserving. So, seeing no material benefit to its inclusion, I have not assigned this pirated version a role in my little Lambert *play*, instead preferring to offer the knowing reader the original source - the fountainhead, if you will - that which opens Volume One of *The Eccentric Mirror*.

The five selections I have chosen showcase Daniel's life from the perspectives of traditional biography, amusing literary sketch, as an author himself, in intimate memoir and as part of celebrated Victorian periodical. Footnotes, scholarly expansions and suggested further reading have all been freely abandoned as, without wishing to repeat myself, these are the oft-quoted primary sources.

There have been some very minor adjustments to punctuation - nothing to harm the integrity of the original texts - but more to account for the prevailing taste and sensibilities of the modern reader. Beyond that, they are as they were when first published.

The true - and immediate - purpose behind this little volume is to ignite a passion for a man I believe has been cruelly overlooked by modern scholars. That he has, for the most part, sunk into oblivion is a wrong that should be righted. And whether by my pen or another's, let us hope that, in the coming years, we'll see a comprehensive, truly authoritative account of this great man's life and legacy enhance bookshops and libraries everywhere.

MB
29th August 2019

THE
Eccentric Mirror:

REFLECTING

A faithful and interesting Delineation of

MALE AND FEMALE CHARACTERS,
ANCIENT AND MODERN,

Who have been particularly distinguished by extraordinary

QUALIFICATIONS, TALENTS, AND PROPENSITIES,

Natural or Acquired,

Comprehending singular Instances of

LONGEVITY,	WONDERFUL EXPLOITS,
CONFORMATION,	ADVENTURES,
BULK,	HABITS,
STATURE,	PROPENSITIES,
POWERS OF MIND AND OF BODY,	ENTERPRISING PURSUITS, &c. &c. &c.

With a faithful Narration of

EVERY INSTANCE OF SINGULARITY,

Manifested in the Lives and Conduct of Characters who have rendered themselves eminently conspicuous by their Eccentricities.

The whole exhibiting an interesting and

WONDERFUL DISPLAY OF HUMAN ACTION

IN THE

Grand Theatre of the World.

Collected and re-collected, from the most authentic Sources,

BY

G. H. WILSON.

IN FOUR VOLUMES.

VOL. I.

London:

PRINTED FOR JAMES CUNDEE,
Ivy-Lane, Paternoster-Row.

1806.

MR. DANIEL LAMBERT
from
THE ECCENTRIC MIRROR
By G.H. WILSON
Printed for James Cundee,
Ivy Lane, Paternoster Row, London
1806

The reader is already aware that the ECCENTRIC MIRROR embraces in its plan memoirs and descriptions of persons remarkable for any extraordinary deviation from the general laws of nature with respect to exterior conformation. Among the living phenomena of this class, none, perhaps, is so deservedly entitled to priority of notice as Mr. Daniel Lambert. Nor is it his astonishing bulk alone that claims for him this distinction. The qualities and endowments of his mind, unoppressed by the vast weight of the body to which it is united, are such as to raise him above the level of the generality of men, and eminently prove that mind is not affected by the modifications of matter. Before we proceed to the particulars of Mr. Lambert's life, we shall indulge in a few reflections, suggested by actual acquaintance and observation.

Mr. Lambert cannot fail to be to every

spectator an object of surprise and wonder, but to the man of science, and especially to the medical practitioner, his peculiarities must be uncommonly interesting. It is impossible to behold his excessive corpulence without being astonished that he was not long ago suffocated by such an accumulation of substance; but when it is known that his breath is perfectly free, and his respiration not in the smallest degree obstructed, even in sleep, that astonishment is proportionately augmented. His voice, indeed, proves that his lungs are as free from oppression as those of any person of the ordinary standard. It might also naturally be supposed that his excessive corpulence was likely to produce a disposition to drowsiness; the reverse is, however, the case. Mr. lambert not only never needs the indulgence of a nap in the daytime, but he exhibits an example of wakefulness truly extraordinary. The perfect and uninterrupted health which he has enjoyed in his progress to his present dimensions, and which he continues to enjoy, is likewise a remarkable trait in the physical history of Mr. Lambert.

While these and other points of equal singularity afford abundant room for speculation to the philosopher, the moralist will delight to investigate the qualities of that mind which animates such a prodigious body. Shrewd and intelligent, Mr. Lambert has improved his natural talents by reading and observation; in company he is lively and agreeable; the general information he possesses, and the numerous anecdotes treasured up in a memory uncommonly retentive, render his society extremely pleasing and instructive. His readiness at repartee, his superiority in characteristic description, and the humorous sallies in which he often indulges, give life, vivacity, and interest, to his conversation. With respect to humanity, temperance, and liberality of sentiment, Mr. Lambert may be held up as a model worthy of general imitation.

The meagre details relative to Mr. Lambert which have hitherto been laid before the public, are equally unsatisfactory and erroneous. This consideration induced the editor of the *Eccentric Mirror* to apply to a source which he knew was not liable to mistake; and as the following is the only authentic account of this remarkable character, he can, with the greater confidence, direct to it the attention of the curious and inquisitive.

Mr. Daniel Lambert was born on the 13th of March 1770, in the Parish of St. Margaret, at Leicester. From the extraordinary bulk to which Mr. Lambert attained, the reader may be naturally disposed to enquire, whether or no his parents were persons of remarkable dimensions. This was not the case; nor were any of his family inclined to corpulence, excepting an uncle and aunt on the father's side, who were both very heavy. The former died during the infancy of Lambert, in the capacity of gamekeeper to the Earl of Stamford, to whose predecessor his father had been huntsman in early life. The family of Lambert, senior, consisted besides Daniel, of another son, who died young, and two daughters, who are still living, and both women of common size.

The habits of the subject of this memoir were not, in any respect, different from those of other young persons till the age of fourteen. Even at that early period he was strongly attached to the sports of the field. This, however, was only the natural effect of a very obvious cause, aided probably by an innate propensity to those diversions. We have already mentioned the profession of his father and uncle and have yet to observe that his maternal grandfather was a great cock-fighter. Born and bred, as it were, among horses, dogs, and cocks, and all the other appendages of sporting, in the pursuits of which he was encouraged, even in his childhood, it cannot be matter of wonder that he should be passionately fond of all those exercises and amusements which are comprehended under the denomination of field sports, as well as of racing, cocking, and fishing.

Brought up under the eye of his parents till the age of fourteen, young Lambert was then placed with Benjamin Patrick, in the manufactory of Taylor & Co. at Birmingham, to learn the business of a die sinker and engraver. This establishment, then one of the most flourishing in that opulent town, was afterwards destroyed in the riots of 1791, by which the celebrated Dr. Priestley was so considerable a sufferer.

Owing to the fluctuations to which all those manufactures that administer to the luxuries of the community are liable from the caprices of fashion, the wares connected with the profession which had been chosen for young

Lambert ceased to be in request. Buckles were all at once proscribed, and a total revolution took place at the same period in the public taste with respect to buttons. The consequence was, that a numerous class of artisans were thrown out of employment and obliged to seek a subsistence in a different occupation. Among these was Lambert, who had then served only four years of his apprenticeship.

Leaving Birmingham, he returned to Leicester to his father, who held the situation of keeper of the prison in that town. Soon afterwards, at the age of nineteen, he began to imagine that he should be a heavy man but had not previously any indications that could lead him to suppose he should ever attain the excessive corpulence for which he was distinguished. He always possessed extraordinary muscular power, and at the time we are speaking of, could lift great weights, and carry five hundred pounds with ease. Had his habits been such as to bring his strength into action, he would doubtless have been an uncommonly powerful man.

That he was not deficient either in physical strength, or in courage, is demonstrated by the following adventure, in which he was about this period engaged.

Standing one day in his father's house at Leicester, his attention was attracted by a company of Savoyards with their dancing dogs and bears, surrounded by an immense concourse of spectators. While they were exhibiting, a dog which had formally been accustomed to travel with a similar company of these grotesque performers, and now belonged to the county gaoler, hearing the sound, flew furiously upon a very large bear, whose overbearing force and weight soon crushed him to the ground. "Give her tooth," said the Savoyards, irritated at the interruption of their exhibition, and making preparations to take off the muzzle of the bear. Mr. Lambert, being acquainted with the master of the dog, and knowing that, in this case, the animal would be exposed to certain destruction, went out and addressed the people, with the intention of pacifying them, and prevailing upon them to suffer the dog to be taken away. Deaf to all his remonstrances, one of the Savoyards still persisted in pulling off the muzzle, the dog being all this time underneath, and in the grasp of the bear. Enraged at the fellow's obstinacy, he protested he would kill the bear if it lay in his power, and snatching from the man's hand the paddle or pole with which they manage these animals, at the moment when the muzzle was removed, he struck the bear with all his force, fully intending to despatch her if possible. Bruin was for a moment completely stunned with the blow, and the dog seized that opportunity of disengaging himself from her clutches. Enraged at this fresh attack, she turned towards her new antagonist, who kept repeating his strokes, but without being able to hit her head, which she protected from his blows with all the dexterity of a most accomplished pugilist. During these successive attacks, the dog, faithful to his friend who had so opportunely stepped to his aid, continued to exhibit the most astonishing proofs of undaunted intrepidity, till he was at length caught up by one of the by-standers. The weather was frosty, and the pavement was slightly glazed from the trundling of a mop. Here, while thus busily engaged in belabouring his formidable foe, Lambert fell, but arose again with the greatest agility. Bruin was now close to him; he had a full view of her tremendous teeth and felt the heat from her breath. The danger became pressing, and as his shaggy foe was too near to admit of his using the weapon, he struck her with his left hand such a violent blow on the skull, as brought her to the ground; on which she declined the contest, and "yelling fled." During the fray, a smaller bear had been standing upright against a wall, with a cocked hat on his head; in consequence of the retreat of his companion, this ludicrous figure now appeared full in front of the victorious champion, who brandished in his hand the up-lifted pole. The beast, as if aware of his danger, and expecting to be attacked in his turn, instantly took off the hat, and, apparently in token of submission, tumbled heels over head at the feet of the conqueror. Meanwhile the populace, terrified at the approach of *ursa major*, began to retire in a backward direction, still keeping the unsuccessful combatant in view, till they tumbled one after another over some loads of coal that happened to lie in the way. The scene now became truly ludicrous: forty people were down at a time; and there was not one but that imagined himself already in the gripe of the irritated animal, vociferated *Murder* with all his might. The Savoyards, who were, after all, the greatest sufferers by this tragi-comic representation, applied to the mayor, and demanded redress. The magistrate enquired where the fray happened and was informed that it took place in Blue Boar Lane, in the parish of St. Nicholas - the inhabitants of which have for many years been distinguished by the appellation of *Nick's Ruffs.* "Oh!" said he, "the people of that parish do just as they please; they are out of my jurisdiction;" and gravely dismissed the disappointed complainants. It was two years before this company of itinerant performers again ventured to make their appearance in Blue Boar Lane. On this occasion, one who happening to be rather before the rest, perceiving Lambert sitting at his door, gave notice to the others, who, dreading a repetition of the treatment they had before experienced, instantly retreated by the way they had come.

It was not very long after the above adventure, that Mr. Lambert experienced an escape from a danger infinitely more alarming, and from the consequences of which no human exertions could possibly have preserved him. He was one of the numerous inhabitants of Leicester, whom the memorable conflagration at the house of a well-known bookseller, now resident in the metropolis, attracted to the spot. It was dark; the fire was then raging in the utmost fury, and Mr. Lambert passed along under a wall, which, from the falling of the others to which it had once been joined, now stood completely detached. When he had reached the extremity, an acquaintance whom he accidently found there, congratulated him on his narrow escape, at the same time pointing to the wall. Lambert, totally unconscious of the risk to which he had been exposed, and now standing in a line with the wall, observed with horror that it rocked to and from like corn in the breeze, and not many moments elapsed, ere it fell with a most tremendous crash.

His father having resigned the office of keeper of the prison, Mr. Lambert succeeded to the situation. It was within a year after this appointment that his bulk received the greatest and most rapid increase. This he attributes to the confinement and sedentary life to which he was now obliged to submit, which produced an effect so much the more striking, as, from his attachment to sporting, he had previously been in the habit of taking a good deal of exercise. Though he never possessed any extraordinary agility, he was still able to kick to the height of seven feet, standing on one leg.

About the year 1793, when Mr. Lambert weighed thirty-two stone, he had occasion to visit Woolwich, in company with the keeper of the county gaol of Leicester. As the tide did not serve to bring them up again to London, he walked from Woolwich to the metropolis, with much less apparent fatigue than several middle-sized men who were of the party.

The inhabitants of Leicester are remarkable for their expertness in swimming, an art which they are encouraged to practice by their vicinity to the river Soar. From the age of eight years Mr. Lambert was an excellent swimmer; and such was his celebrity, that about ten years ago, all the young people in his native town, who were learning to swim, resorted to him for instruction. His power of floating, owing to his uncommon bulk, was so great, that he could swim with two men of ordinary size upon his back. We have heard him relate, that on these occasions, when any of his young pupils manifested any timidity, he would convey them to the opposite bank of the river from that on which they laid their clothes, and there leave them to find their way back as well as they could. By these means they soon acquired that courage which is so indispensably necessary to the attainment of excellence in the art of swimming.

Mr. Lambert's father died about five years after his son's appointment to be keeper of the prison, which office he held till Easter 1805. In this situation he manifested a disposition fraught with humanity and benevolence. Whatever severity he might be under the necessity of exercising towards the unhappy objects committed to his care during their confinement, he never forebore to make the greatest exertions to assist them at the time of their trials. Few left the prison without testifying their gratitude, and tears often bespoke the sincerity of the feelings they expressed. His removal from the office was in consequence of a wish on the part of the magistrates to employ the prisoners in the manufacture of the town. As a proof of the approbation which his conduct had merited, they settled upon him an annuity of £50 for life, without any solicitation whatever; and, what was still more gratifying to his feelings, this grant was accompanied with a declaration, that it was a mark of their esteem, and of the universal satisfaction which he had given in the discharge of the duties of his office.

Such were the feelings of Mr. Lambert, that, no longer than a year ago, he abhorred the very idea of exhibiting himself. Though he lived exceedingly retired in Leicester, the fame of his uncommon corpulence had spread over the adjacent country to such a degree, that he frequently found himself not a little incommoded by the curiosity of the people, which it was impossible to repress, and which they were continually devising the means of gratifying, in spite of his reluctance.

A gentleman travelling through Leicester conceived a strong desire to see this extraordinary phenomenon; but, being at a loss for a pretext to introduce himself to Mr. Lambert, he first took care to enquire what were his particular propensities. Being informed that he was a great cocker, the traveller thought himself sure of success. He accordingly went to his house, knocked at the door, and enquired for Mr. Lambert. The servant answered that he was at home, but that he never saw strangers. "Let him know," replied the curious traveller, "that I called about some cocks." Lambert, who chanced to be in a situation to overhear what passed, immediately re-joined: "Tell the gentleman that I am a *shy* cock."

On another occasion, a gentleman from Nottingham was extremely importunate to see him, pretending that he had a particular favour to ask. After considerable hesitation, Mr. Lambert directed him to be admitted. On being introduced, he said he wished to enquire the pedigree of a certain mare. "Oh! if that's all," replied Mr. Lambert, perceiving, from his manner, the real nature of his errand, "she was got by Impertinence out of Curiosity."

Finding, at length, that he must either submit to be a close prisoner in his own house or endure all the inconveniences without receiving any of the profits of an exhibition, Mr. Lambert wisely strove to overcome his repugnance, and determined to visit the metropolis for that purpose. As it was impossible to procure a carriage large enough to admit him, he had a vehicle constructed expressly to convey him to London, where he arrived, for the twenty-second time, in the spring of 1806, and fixed his residence at Piccadilly.

His apartments there had more the air of a

place of fashionable resort, than of an exhibition; and, as long as the town continued full, he was visited by a great deal of the best company. The dread he felt on coming to London, lest he should be exposed to indignity and insult from the curiosity of some of his visitors, was soon removed by the politeness and attention which he universally experienced. There was not a gentleman in town from his own county, but went to see him, not merely gazing at him as a spectacle, but treating him in the most friendly and soothing manner, which, he has declared, is too deeply impressed upon his mind ever to be forgotten.

The spirit of politeness which always prevailed in the presence of Mr. Lambert, was such as, was, perhaps, never observed on a similar occasion. The very Quakers by whom he was visited felt themselves *moved* to take off their hats. It is but natural to suppose that among the numbers who chose to gratify their curiosity, some few exceptions should occur. Thus, one day a person perceiving, previous to entering the room, that the company were uncovered, observed to Mr. Lambert's attendant, that he would not take off his hat, even if the king were present. This rude remark being uttered in the hearing of Mr. Lambert, he immediately replied, as the stranger entered:- "Then by G-----, Sir, you must instantly quit this room, as I do not consider it as a mark of respect due to myself, but to the ladies and gentlemen who honour me with their company."

Many of the visitors seemed incapable of gratifying their curiosity to its full extent, and called again and again to behold to what an immense magnitude the human figure is capable of attaining; nay, one gentleman, a banker in the City, jocosely observed, that he had fairly had a pound's worth.

Mr. Lambert had the pleasure of receiving persons of all descriptions and of all nations. He was one day visited by a party of fourteen, eight ladies and six gentlemen, who expressed their joy at not being too late, as it was near the time of closing the door for the day. They assured him that they had come from Guernsey on purpose to convince themselves of the existence of such a prodigy as Mr. Lambert had been described to be by one of their neighbours, who had seen him; adding, that they had not even one single friend or acquaintance in London, so that they had no other motive whatever for their voyage. A striking illustration of the power of curiosity over the human mind.

Great numbers of foreigners were gratified with the contemplation of a spectacle, unequalled, perhaps, in any other country. Among these a Frenchman, accompanied by a Jew, seemed extremely desirous, from motives best known to himself, of persuading Mr. Lambert to make an excursion to the continent, and insinuating that under his guidance and management he could not fail of obtaining the greatest success. "Vy you not go to France?" said he, "I am sure Buonaparte vil make your fortune." Supposing that such an inducement must prove irresistible, he added: "Den vont you go to Paris?" Lambert, who had too much good sense to be the dupe of a designing *Monsieur*, re-joined in the emphatic style of a true son of John Bull, "If I do, I'll be d----d." "Vat you think of dat now?" cried the astonished Jew to his mortified and disappointed companion.

Among the many visitors of Mr. Lambert the celebrated Polish dwarf, Count Borulawski was not the least interesting. The Count, having made a fortune by exhibiting his person, has retired to Durham to enjoy the fruit of his economy. Though now in his seventy-first year, he still possesses all the gracefulness and vivacity by which he was formerly characterized. Mr. Lambert, during his apprenticeship at Birmingham, went several times to see Borulawski, and such was the strength of the Count's memory, that he had scarcely fixed his eyes upon him in Piccadilly before he recollected his face. After reflecting a moment, he exclaimed that he had seen his face twenty years ago in Birmingham, but it was not surely the same body. This unexpected meeting of the largest and smallest man seemed to realise the fabled history of the inhabitants of Lilliput and Brobdingnag, particularly when Lambert rose for the purpose of affording the diminutive Count a full view of his prodigious dimensions. In the course of conversation, Mr. Lambert asked what quantity of cloth the Count required for a coat, and how many he thought his would make him. "Not many;" answered Borulawski. "I take goot large piece cloth myself - almost tree quarters of yard." At this rate, one of Mr. Lambert's sleeves would be abundantly sufficient for the purpose. The Count felt one of Mr. Lambert's legs: "Ah mine

Got!" he exclaimed, "pure flesh and blood. I feel de warm. No deception! I am pleased: for I did hear it was deception." Mr. Lambert asked if his lady was alive; on which he replied "No, she is dead, and (putting his finger significantly to his nose) I am not very sorry, for when I affronted her, she put me on the mantle-shelf for punishment."

The many characters that introduced themselves to Mr. Lambert's observation in the metropolis furnished him with a great number of anecdotes, which a retentive memory enables him to relate to good effect.

One day, the room being rather crowded with company, a young man in the front, almost close to Mr. Lambert, made incessant use of one of those indispensable appendages of a modern beau, called a quizzing glass. The conversation turned on the changes in the weather, and in what manner Mr. Lambert felt himself affected by them. "What do you dislike most?" asked the beau. "To be bored with a quizzing glass," was the reply.

A person asking him in a very rude way the cost of one of his coats, he returned him no answer. The man repeated the question with the observation, that he thought he had a right to demand any information, having contributed his shilling, which would help to pay for Mr. Lambert's coat as well as the rest. "Sir," re-joined Lambert, "if I knew what part of my next coat your shilling would pay for, I can assure you I would cut out the piece."

On another occasion a lady was particularly solicitous to have the same question resolved. "Indeed, Madam," answered Mr. Lambert, "I cannot pretend to charge my memory with the price, but I can put you into a method of obtaining the information you want. If you think it proper to make me a present of a new coat, you will then know exactly what it costs."

A person, who had the appearance of a gentleman, one day took the liberty of asking several impertinent questions. Mr. Lambert looked him sternly in the face, but without making any reply. A lady now entered the room, and Lambert entered into conversation with her, on which the same person observed that he was more polite to ladies than to gentlemen. "I can assure you, Sir," answered Mr. Lambert, "that I consider it my duty to treat with equal politeness all those whose behaviour convinces me that they are gentlemen." "I suppose," re-joined the querist, "you mean to infer that I am no gentleman." "That I certainly did," was the reply. Not yet abashed by this reproof, he soon afterwards ventured to ask another question, of a similar nature with the preceding. Irritated at these repeated violations of decency, which bespoke a deficiency of good sense as well as good manners, Mr. Lambert fixed his eyes full upon the stranger, "You came into this room, Sir, by the door, but-----" "You mean to say," continued the other, looking at the window, "that I may possibly make my exit by some other way." "Begone this moment," thundered Lambert, "or by G-d I'll throw you into Piccadilly." No second injunction was necessary to rid him of this obnoxious guest.

After a residence of about five months in the metropolis, where we believe his success was fully adequate to his most sanguine expectations, Mr. Lambert returned in September 1806, to his native town.

We shall now proceed to state what we have been able to collect relative to the habits, manners, and propensities, of this extraordinary man.

It is not improbable that incessant exercise in the open air, in the early part of his life, laid the foundation of an uncommonly healthy constitution. Mr. Lambert scarcely knew what it was to be ailing or indisposed. His temperance, no doubt, contributed towards this uninterrupted flow of health. His food differed in no respect from that of other people: he ate with moderation, and of one dish only at a time. He never drank any other beverage than water, and though at one period of his life he seldom spent an evening at home, but with convivial parties, he never could be prevailed upon to join his companions in their libations to the jolly god. One of the qualifications that strongly tended to promote harmony and conviviality was possessed in an eminent degree by Mr. Lambert. He had a fine, powerful, melodious voice. It was a strong tenor, unlike that of a fat man, light and unembarrassed, and the articulation perfectly clear.

Mr Lambert's height was five feet eleven inches, and in June 1805, he had attained the enormous weight of fifty stone, four pounds. He never felt any pain in his progress towards his greatest bulk but increased gradually and imperceptibly.

Before he grew bulky, he never knew what it

was to be out of wind. It is evident to all those who were acquainted with him, that he had no oppression on the lungs from fat, or any other cause; and Dr. Heaviside has expressed his opinion that his life was as good as that of any other healthy man. He conceived himself that he could walk a quarter of a mile, was able to go upstairs with great ease, and without inconvenience, and notwithstanding his excessive corpulence, could not only stoop without trouble to write, but even kept up an extensive correspondence, insomuch that his writing table resembled the desk of a merchant's counting-house.

Mr. Lambert slept less than the generality of mankind, being never more than eight hours in bed. He was never inclined to drowsiness either after dinner, or in any other part of the day; and such was the vivacity of his disposition, that he was always the last person to retire to rest, which he never did before one o'clock. He slept without having his head raised more than is usual with other men, and always with the window open. His respiration was so perfectly free and unobstructed, that he never snored, and what is not a little extraordinary, he could awake within five minutes of any time he pleased. All the secretions were carried on in him with the same facility as in any other person.

We have already adverted to Mr. Lambert's fondness for hunting, coursing, racing, fishing, and cocking. He was likewise well-known in his neighbourhood as a great otter-hunter. Till within these few years he was extremely active in all the sports of the field, and though he was prevented by his corpulence from partaking in them, he still bred cocks, setters, and pointers, which he had brought to as great, or perhaps greater, perfection than any other sporting character of the present day. At the time when terriers were the vogue, he possessed no less than thirty of them at once. The high estimation in which the animals of his breeding were held by sporting amateurs, was fully evinced in the sale of the dogs which he brought with him to London, and which were disposed of at Tattersall's at the following prices: Peg, a black setter bitch, forty-one guineas; Punch, a setter dog, twenty-six guineas; Brush, ditto, seventeen guineas; Bob, ditto, twenty guineas; Bounce, ditto, twenty-two guineas; Sam, ditto, twenty-six guineas; Bell, ditto, thirty-two guineas; Charlotte, a pointer bitch, twenty-two guineas; Lucy, ditto, twelve guineas. Total, 218 guineas. Mr. Mellish was the purchaser of the seven setters, and Lord Kinnaird of the two pointers.

If Mr. Lambert had a greater attachment to one kind of sport than another, it was to racing, for which he always manifested a peculiar preference. He was fond of riding himself, before his weight prevented him from enjoying that exercise; and it was his opinion, founded on experience, that the more blood and the better a horse was bred, the better he carried him.

During his residence in London, Mr. Lambert found himself in no wise affected by the change of air, unless he ought to attribute to that cause an occasional, momentary, trifling depression of spirits in a morning, such as he had felt on his recovery from inflammatory attacks, which were the only kind of indisposition he ever remembered to have experienced.

The extraordinary share of health he enjoyed was not the result of any unusual precaution on his part, as he had in many instances accustomed himself to the total neglect of those means by which men in general endeavour to preserve that inestimable blessing. As a proof of this the following fact is related from his own lips. Before his increasing size prevented his partaking in the sports of the field, he never could be prevailed upon, when he returned home at night from these excursions, to change any part of his clothes, however wet they might be; and he put them on again the next morning, though they were perhaps so thoroughly soaked, as to leave behind them their mark on the floor. Notwithstanding this, he never knew what it was to take a cold. On one of these occasions he was engaged with a party of young men in a boat, in drawing a pond. Knowing that a principal part of this diversion always consists in sousing each other as much as possible, Lambert, before he entered the boat, walked, in his clothes, up to his chin into the water. He remained there the whole of the day in this condition, which to any other man must have proved intolerably irksome. At night, on retiring to bed, he stripped off his shirt and all, and the next morning, putting on his clothes again, wet as they were, he resumed the diversion with the rest of his companions. Nor was this all; for lying down in the bottom of the boat, he took a comfortable nap for a couple of hours, and though the weather was rather severe, he experienced no kind of inconvenience from what might justly be considered as extreme indiscretion.

It would have been an interesting speculation to try how far a certain regimen might tend to reduce Mr. Lambert's excessive bulk, which, however healthy he might be, could but be productive of some inconvenience, besides depriving him of enjoyments to which he was passionately attached. The annals of medicine furnish a very remarkable instance of this sort, and though the person bore no resemblance, except in bulk, to Mr. Lambert, yet the analogy is sufficiently striking to induce a belief that the adoption of a similar method would be attended with similar effects. The case to which we allude is that of Mr. Thomas Wood, a miller, of Billericay, in Essex, which is related in the second volume of Medical Transactions by Sir George Baker. Mr. Wood, after passing the preceding part of his life in eating and drinking without weight or measure, found himself, in the year 1764, and in the 45th year of his age, overwhelmed with the complication of the most painful and terrible disorders. In the catalogue were comprehended frequent sickness of the stomach, pain in the bowels, headache and vertigo; he had an almost constant thirst, a great lowness of spirits, fits of the gravel, violent rheumatism, and frequent attacks of the gout, also two epileptic fits. To this copious list of diseases were added, a formidable sense of suffocation, particularly after meals, and an extreme corpulence of person. On reading the life of Carnaro, recommended to his perusal by the Rev. Mr. Powley, a worthy clergyman in his neighbourhood, he immediately formed a resolution to follow the salutary precepts inculcated and exemplified in that performance. He prudently, however, did not make a sudden change in his manner of living; after proper gradations both with respect to the quantity and quality of his meat and drink, he finally left off the use of all fermented liquors on the 4th of January 1765, when he commenced water-drinking. He did not even long indulge himself even in this last innocent beverage; for on the 25th of October following, having accidentally dined that day without drinking, he finally took his leave of that and every other kind of drink not having tasted a single drop of any liquor whatsoever, excepting only what he had occasionally taken in the form of medicine, and two glasses and a half of water drank on the 9th of May 1766, from that date till August 22, 1771, the day on which Sir George Baker drew up this account.

With respect to solid nutriment, the 31st of 1767, was the last time of his eating any kind of animal food. In its room he substituted a single dish, of which he made only two meals in the twenty-four hours; one at four or five in the morning, and the other at noon. This consisted of pudding, (of which he eat a pound and a half,) made of three pints of skimmed milk, poured boiling hot on a pound of sea-biscuit overnight, to which two eggs were added next morning, and the whole boiled in a cloth about an hour. Finding this diet too nutritious, and having grown fat during the use of it, he threw out the eggs and milk, and formed a new edition of pudding, consisting only of a pound of coarse flour, and a pint of water boiled together. He was at first much delighted with this new recipe, and lived upon it three months; but finding it not easily digestible, he finally formed a mess, which ever afterwards constituted the whole of his nourishment, composed of a pound of the best flour, boiled to a proper stiffness with a pint and a half of skimmed milk, without any other addition.

Such was the regimen of diet, as agreeable to his palate as his former food used to be, by means of which, with a considerable share of exercise, Mr. Wood got rid of the encumbrance of ten or eleven stone of distempered flesh and fat; and, to use his own expression, "was metamorphosed from a monster to a person of moderate size: from the condition of an unhealthy decrepit old man, to perfect health, and to the vigour and activity of youth;" his spirits lively, his sleep undisturbed, and his strength of muscles so far improved, that he could carry a quarter of a ton weight, which he in vain attempted to perform when he was about the age of thirty, and in perfect health.

We leave to medical men to decide what would be the probable result of a like procedure with respect to Mr. Lambert; but, for our own part, we cannot forbear thinking that, with his healthy constitution and less advanced age, its consequences would be infinitely more striking and beneficial.

We here take our leave of Mr. lambert, for

whom, as undoubtedly the *greatest* man in the British empire, the first place in our gallery will not be thought inappropriate. The term *greatest* will not, it is presumed, be thought misapplied when it is known that he measured three yards four inches round the body, and one yard one inch, round the leg, and that a suit of his clothes cost about twenty pounds.

THE

ENGLISH ANNUAL,

FOR

MDCCCXXXVIII.

> Whoever thinks a faultless piece to see,
> Thinks what ne'er was, nor is, nor e'er shall be.
> In every work regard the writer's end,
> Since none can compass more than they intend;
> And if the means be just, the conduct true,
> Applause, in spite of trivial faults, is due.
> POPE. ESSAY ON CRITICISM.

LONDON:
PUBLISHED BY EDWARD CHURTON,
26, HOLLES STREET, CAVENDISH SQUARE.

MDCCCXXXVIII.

from
THE ENGLISH ANNUAL
For MDCCCXXXVIII
By OMEGA
Published by Edward Churton
1838

SOME ACCOUNT OF THE LATE DANIEL LAMBERT, ESQ.

With Selections from his Papers

It was not chance but destiny that directed me to an inn, yclept the Waggon and Horses, at Stamford. A sense of being carried off my feet and wafted into the passage remains with me to this day. I feel that it was at that moment destined that I should be exalted into the dignity of editorial biographer. I was to be set up in type - Mr. Heber was to be curious concerning me - Mr. Dyce was to hazard the chance of an introduction - Earl Spencer was to hang at my skirts imploringly - "Four-and-twenty booksellers all in a Row" were to be anxious overmuch in their inquiries after me - I was to be a collector of MSS. - a presentiment of these coming honours attending me as I entered the inn at Stamford.

A pair of slippers had made me their temporary proprietor - or rather, as Dr. Johnson, my great predecessor, might have said, I had autocratically subpedified them - I had adjusted by wig so that mine ears might be permitted to exercise their auricular privileges without restraint - I had quelled, by the gratuity of a steak, that wolf in the stomach which, in spite of the assertion that such race of animals is extinct in this country, I contend every Englishman possesses in his interior humanity; and I had just drawn out of the fender a bottle of port, which the fire had thawed into a vinous viper that was to tickle me into ecstasy.

A thought occurred - was I to spend the evening alone? It is true that I was comfortable enough for the present - and a long vista of delight, extending from eight o'clock till midnight, lay stretched before, at the extremity of which, tumblers of brandy and water were dancing with fantastic motion. But a sensation of uneasiness pervaded me, nevertheless; and the coach by which I had arrived from London had contracted itself into the smallest possible dimensions, and had taken an inside place in my head, where it was driving along to the infinite vexation of that small portion of intellectuality which, for lack of a more appropriate title, I must dignify by the appellation of brains. I felt, also, with painful certainty, that I was alone. I would have hailed the presence of a double-tongued octogenarian, "full of anecdote, and with *such* a surprising memory" - I would have welcomed a Benthamite or a Utilitarian - I should have been glad of the company of Mr. Zimmerman - after supper. "Oh solitude, romantic maid!" thou who, like many other young ladies, art *so* interesting, but *so* silent, - let us invite a third. I arose and rang for the landlord.

There was a sort of Boniface obeisance as the host entered the room, that plainly shadowed forth the approaching landlord, with a kind of vague touch-and-go harmony of discourse as we fell into conversation, indicating a consciousness that he was, as it is termed, playing second fiddle. But, as the wine circulated nimbly through his physical economy, mine host began to wax facetious; and his system, as well colloquial as corporate, underwent a genial glow no less surprising than agreeable.

"Pray, sir," said he, surveying me with the experienced eye of a connoisseur, "may I make so bold as to inquire your weight?"

"A strange question, indeed, most curious vintner," I exclaimed, with that urbane smile for which I am distinguished - "but I will e'en gratify you: - I believe, if steelyard or scale say true, it will pronounce me about twenty stone."

"A very pretty weight," replied the landlord, with a gravity of countenance peculiarly appropriate to the subject: "but ah! Sir, you are not, perhaps, aware that in this very room Mr. Daniel Lambert breathed his last."

I had often heard of Daniel Lambert, that "truly great man," whose vast proprietorship of fat had been the wonder and delight of his contemporaries: and I felt, I trust, a becoming awe when it was signified to me that that remarkable individual had made his exit through one side of the room in which I was then reposing myself.

"Mr. Lambert, sir," resumed the host, "was a very cheerful and pleasant companion; and often let fall good things, considered trifles by himself, which others appropriated to themselves and passed off as their own."

"Very likely," said I - "we know not, landlord, how much of our own hair is woven into another man's wig;" and I arranged my own with the air of one who conceives that he has delivered himself of a profound remark.

"Ha! Ha! very true," cried the host, wondering what the deuce I could mean; "but I suppose, sir, you never heard that Mr. Lambert was an author?"

"An author! I certainly was never given to understand that he possessed literary attainments."

"Oh! dear yes," cried mine host - "I don't know whether Mr. Lambert was ever in print, but I have by me a great number of papers which were left behind him when he died."

Daniel Lambert a literary character! It was strange - it was passing strange, - it was wonderful. I fell into a reverie. I speculated upon the subjects likely to be entertained by the author. Of what could he possibly have written? Of whom? Was it an epic poem or a tragedy, - was it a satire, or a collection of songs - elegies or odes - epigram or lampoon? But no. - Lambert must have delighted in the lugubriously vast - in the morosely magnificent - in the extensively terrible. Himself a human and vital Mont Blanc - his genius must be Alpine - he must have composed a treatise on the infinity of space - or prepared a dissertation on the pyramids - or have employed his hand upon the Andes, Teneriffe, or Atlas. Taking the cue from Gibbon, had he completed a history of the *Fati*mites? Whatever it might be, I felt assured that it would prove worthy of his greatness. Far removed from the vulgar herd of base and hungry scribes, who like fretful porcupines, are perpetually shooting their quills at each other, I was satisfied that Lambert would be found no vulgar quill-driver.

"Can I be permitted a glance at these MSS. in your possession?" I demanded of the landlord, awaking from the reverie into which I had fallen.

"Surely, sir, surely," answered the host as he bustled from the room - returning presently with a small bundle of papers neatly folded, and carefully tied together with a piece of red tape.

I confess that the first cursory view of the papers, as they still lay in the hands of the landlord, somewhat disappointed me. I had looked for something of a more imposing description. I took it for granted that elephant foolscap was the approved size of Mr.

Lambert's note-paper - and I expected that his literary lucubrations would require to be unfurled like the mysterious scroll of a magician in the pantomime. I conceived it probable that he literally wrote on sheets of paper - with a pen plucked from the pinion of a griffin, and with ink obtained, forsooth, from the boiling pool of Phlegethon. No such thing. Mr. Lambert luxuriated in an inimitably beautiful Italian hand - such a hand as Mr. Keightley may be supposed to have adopted when he wrote his delightful "Fairy Mythology" - apparently with a crow-quill, and on gilt-edged Bath paper.

I had not, however, gone far in the perusal of Daniel Lambert's remains, when I turned suddenly towards the landlord, and offered him a round sum for the whole collection. The precise sum I tendered - which mine host incontinently and with inexpressible gratification accepted - must remain an inviolable secret between him and myself. Enough to hint that it was immense; calculated to show my sense of the merits of the author, and, at the same time, to convince the immediately prior possessor that I was far above vulgar considerations of profit and loss in a matter involving the personal fame of the immense defunct. My sole object, I am proud to own, in the editing of these remains, was to acquire for their gifted author - a niche, shall I say? - no - that were uncomfortably to cramp and to confine him - a huge recess in the temple of Fame.

But, before I proceed to select specimens of these invaluable relics, which I bathe from morn to night in tears of heartfelt ecstasy and joy - let me, as is the custom of fond and painstaking editors, furnish the excited reader with a biographical notice of the writer, obtained from a careful and strict examination of surviving friends, whose testimony has been sedulously sifted, contrasted, and compared, and from the contemporary notices of respectable compilers for the authentic obituary. Lambert must not be suffered to sink into oblivion like "the fat weed that rots on Lethe's wharf." Be it, on the contrary, the peculiar care of his biographer to clear him from the quay in the most triumphant and satisfactory manner possible.

Daniel Lambert, then, was born at Leicester in the year 1770; evincing at his birth no striking peculiarities of conformation sufficient to indicate or announce his future greatness. But as the past happens to be a rather reserved lady, wearing a very black veil, we shall not be rude or ungallant enough to attempt to raise it; and must, therefore, commit his infancy to that transient notice which will be sufficient to satisfy the reader of our belief that he was once really an infant - a small babe - the minute seed of the future pumpkin - the insignificant acorn that expanded into the important oak - a mouse out of which crept a mountain. Suffice it to say, that "he grew, and he grew, and he grew" - and continued to grow, till his parents, relations and friends, began verily to think that *Grotius*, and *Puffendorff*, and *Vattel* had been born again, and that the youthful Lambert was destined to figure in the world as a great jurisconsult. Not he. He knew and cared nothing about international law - he was a universe of himself - a vast continent - a new world of flesh. "The fattest hog in Epicurus' sty" was but a suckling pig compared with him. "Leviathan that swims the ocean stream," when Lambert bathed, looked little, and thus was ashamed.

At twenty-three years of age, he was thirty-two stone, or four hundred and forty-eight pounds in weight - but active, nimble, volatile -

full of quips, cranks, conceits, and national vagaries; springing over the cold impediments of custom, like a vaulting walrus playing at leapfrog with an iceberg, and bounding over the high-raised heads of a stiff-necked generation, like a fun-fraught elephant jumping over the summit of a camelopard.

But his youth was highly blighted. Lambert fell in love with an impracticable widow; and sighed, "not like a furnace," but like all furnaces between Birmingham and Wolverhampton. That obdurate fair, however, did what very few beside could have done - she made *light* of him - held him as nought - and, in fine, rejected his addresses. He never knelt before her, it is true, for where was the lever of Archimedes? and he perhaps remembered the false position in which Gibbon had placed himself on a similar occasion - which Mr. Leigh Hunt, we think, facetiously designated "The Decline and Fall;" but he proposed to make her his *better half* (poor, short-sighted man!) in the most delicate and respectful manner. Did he fall away upon this strangulation of his young hopes? The question is natural. No. On the contrary, he rose away at an incredible rate. Stung to madness by this rejection of his proffered suit, he swelled out of all reasonable compass.

By this time the world began to be astir about him. What was the man at? The folks of Leicester marvelled greatly and wondered how all this was to end. Lean and slippered pantaloons laid their heads together at the corners of streets and muttered strange complaints of monopoly. The Leicester prize ox swooned with envy and mortification when it beheld his far superior vastness. His house was infested by visitors, high, low, and of all degrees, and of every description. One, more cunning in contrivance than the rest, hoped to obtain an introduction to the huge Chimæra by sending in word through the medium of the servant, that he came to purchase some cocks, of which Lambert was the proprietor. "Tell him," quoth Lambert, who, having squeezed himself behind the folding doors of the parlour, had overheard the impertinent applicant, "Tell him I am a shy cock!"

A thought found its way into the brain of Lambert; it was a natural, proper, and profitable thought. "If," (such was the train of his argument) - "if I am so worthy of being viewed, why not make people pay for peeping?" He accordingly resolved on taxing the eyes of the community; and as bears are known to retire for the winter, and to subsist upon their acquired fat, in like manner did Daniel Lambert propose to make his own fat serve as a means of subsistence for the winter of his days. Behold him, then, drawn in a carriage made expressly for him, and conveyed to London, where he arrived in September 1806, fixing his quarters (all of them) at a house in Piccadilly.

Here, during the space of three years, he was waited upon by an immense assemblage of rank, fashion, and beauty. Ministers, peers, foreign ambassadors, and civil functionaries crowded to his daily levee. Mr. Pitt had seen him in the country a year or two before, and being now dead was, of course, unable to see him again; but his remark respecting him deserves to be recorded: he said that "he had increased, was increasing, and ought to be diminished." Mr. Fox, whose curiosity had been excited by rumours of his greatness, came, a short time previous to his death, to wait upon him. That great man avowed his belief that Mr. Lambert was of himself a general meeting - an incorporated society - a consolidated mob; and said, that he alone would constitute a deputation from the English people. Mr. Sheridan whispered in the ear of the friend who accompanied him an arithmetical problem to this effect: - if Ariel could put a girdle round the earth in forty minutes, how long would she be in placing a belt around Mr. Lambert? He was pleased to inquire, also, whether Mr. Lambert was fond of music; and being answered in the affirmative, protested that he would send him a violoncello to play upon, which he trusted would serve by way of kit. He remarked that, without disparagement to Mr. Lambert's spiritual magnitude, his soul must be like a dwarf sitting alone in the middle of St. Peter's at Rome; and when he took his leave, was heard kindly to express his determination, so long as Mr. Lambert remained *in the flesh*, to come and visit him. The court of aldermen, when first their eyes did rest upon him, turned green with envy, like the fat of turtles; and looked like very small shrimps gazing at a very large lobster.

But know all England was hoarse with calling him to her several localities; and panting horseflesh toiled before him, drawing, and tearing, and tugging, and lugging him about the kingdom. At length, from Huntingdon he has removed to Stamford, and, like an honourable and punctual man, paid the carrier his tonnage on the instant; and, now, what did he do? He knew when he first came to London, that no common inn would receive him. He knew full well that the "Goat in Boots" would have taken to its heels like Jack the Giant-Killer newly shod in his seven leaguers; and that the "Cat and Bagpipes" would together have raised such a discordant and excruciating din at his approach as would have alarmed the neighbourhood. He was certain that the "Bull and Mouth" when it beheld him, would have looked all mouth and no bull; and that the "Belle Sauvage" would have turned into the "Saracen's Head" immediately he made his appearance at the gate. Accordingly, when he arrived at Stamford, he wisely chose to domiciliate himself at an inn appropriately termed the "Waggon and Horses." Here, accommodated with a ground floor - to rise would have been ruin, for any attempt to bring him up must have had the inevitable effect of bringing down the stairs - he prepared with a cheerful heart to see company; sending his compliments to the Editor of the Stamford

Mercury, and requesting that, "as the mountain could not wait upon Mahomet, Mahomet would come to the mountain." The Mahomet, who came in the shape of a printer's devil, took Mr. Lambert's orders to announce his arrival in the next paper, and retired blessing himself, and much marvelling how that very, very great gentleman would be able to get up to the seventh heaven. Before the following day, however, the soul of Lambert was on its way thither; he was found dead in his bed early on the next morning, to the inexpressible joy of the bed posts and sacking; which during the night, as he turned and tumbled about, had been shrieking most wildly.

Thus, at the age of forty, on the 21st of July * 1809, died Daniel Lambert; of whom (to press into our service a quotation which we think was never employed before) we may truly say,

*"Take him for all in all,
We ne'er shall look upon his like again."*

A man, or rather a vast human vessel, who, when he was last under weigh, told by the scale the miraculous weight of fifty-two stone eleven, or seven hundred and thirty-nine pounds; being ten stone eleven pounds more than the great Mr. Bright of Maldon, and almost as heavy as an epic poem. - Shall we moralise over the deceased? No, we will not disturb the dust - (almost as huge a pile, we imagine, as the vast heap formally at Battle Bridge) by paltry and miserable rankings after matters, good or bad, that might be picked out of it.

Upon once more looking over the papers of Mr. Lambert, from which I propose to gratify the grateful reader with a small selection (for I intended publishing the whole shortly in two quarto volumes), I cannot help feeling and lamenting the difficulty of making such a bouquet as shall at once satisfy the public of the author's claims for immortality, and present, at the same time, a fair specimen of the prolific garden from which it has been culled. I am aware that I sometimes do not even offer a brick as a sample of the edifice I am about to erect; and that what I may, perchance, conceive to be an exquisitely carved cornice may, to other eyes, appear nothing better than a piece of rough wood: others may deem these delightful recreations laborious nothings; others may say,

> *"They seem not like the ruins of his youth,*
> *But like the ruins of those ruins."*

I opine that they are palaces of adamant, such as a literary Palladio or Vitruvius might be proud to acknowledge.

There is one prominent feature on the face of these effusions, - they distinctively relate to self. He squeezes himself into the smallest compositions; there is a morbidness of feeling that Byron himself might have envied or approved. Thus, though he sometimes extols his double-extra corpulence, he not unfrequently desponds grievously; although at times he is a Falstaff in jovial geniality, he occasionally is a Master Slender in sentiment.

Take for example the following melancholy madrigal, in which

> *"The burden and the mystery*
> *Of all this unintelligible world"*

are most feelingly and pathetically deplored. The sympathetic reader will perceive that the unhappy man meditates self-slaughter - of such contradictory elements is human nature composed; but man is an anomaly!

* *Daniel Lambert died on 21st of JUNE (not July) 1809 - Editor*

LAMBERT'S LAMENT

"Oh! that this too, too solid flesh would melt,
Thaw, and resolve itself into Adieu!"
Shakespeare

I wish I were where Falstaff lies,
For I am tired of lingering here,
And every hour affliction cries
Go - and partake his not small bier.

I wish I could; for I am sick
Of all this fatness round about;
Thick-coming fancies make me thick,
And stout objections made me stout.

I weep - it only puffs my cheeks,
I sigh - it only swells me more;
I get quite lusty on my shrieks,
I'm all the fatter for my roar.

The ocean tide that ebbs and flows, -
The stars that twinkle in the sky, -
The early day that comes and goes, -

All these move nimbly - so don't I.

I dream'd an oriental dream,
As on my bed of down I lay!
I sigh, for Fatima's my theme;
And while I keep this fat I may.

Oh! could I close this scene of care;
Oh! were I quietly inurn'd;
Oh! would I could vacate the chair;
Oh! might this meeting be adjourned!

I'll beg a cannon from a friend;
I'll get a cable strong and tough;
A kitchen spit my woes might end,
But, oh! it's not half long enough.

The three exquisite poems, which we are now about to extract, display our author in a very different light. He has dedicated them to several friends. Lambert, like other great poets, knew that by linking the name of a friend to one of his poems, however small, he should confer an everlasting obligation - for immortality is the portion of these delicate but perennial blossoms. The first is addressed:

TO MR. WOOLLEY

A SONNET.

How little tender lamb, in frisking glee,
While on the sward so green with future crops,
Dancing about the glade with nimble hops,
Thou guessest what thy future fate will be!

Thou fleece upon a great stout man I see;
Thy leg upon a well-laid table drops;
Thy head is broth, thy ribs are mutton chops;
Thou art but active mutton unto me.

So yonder bellowing ox that swells with grief,
So yonder calf that piles the awkward heel,
One would not answer to the name of beef,
The other does not know his name is veal.
Alas! From thee I learn this lesson just,
That Lambert's not thy name, but Daniel Dust.

The next is worthy of Mr. Wordsworth. It shows how easily a man of genius can elevate trifles into importance.

TO DR. BUZZBY

ON A TROUBLESOME BLUEBOTTLE TORMENTING THE AUTHOR

Fly not yet; 'tis now the hour
When vile dyspepsia wields her pow'r,
And I would close mine eyes, and doze
  Like that great sloth of Polito's.

Tell me no more my cheeks are made
  To be a level fly-parade,
For country dance or spinning waltz,
Or all that flyhood's youth exalts.

Tell me no more my nose is form'd
  To be by tilting midges storm'd;
Or that mine ears shall serve as dens
  For thy absconding citizens.

Tell me no more thou hoverest near,
  To be soft music to mine ear;
Tell me no more that thou dost come
  To sing to me - it's all a hum.

The third of these delightful little pieces is somewhat similar to the preceding. There is, however, a truculent turn at the conclusion which seems to indicate that the author was in one of those irritable fits to which men of genius are particularly, indeed, proverbially, subject.

TO ---- WEB-STIR, ESQ.

ON A SPIDER

When Edward went the Welsh to mow,
    Of danger a derider,
With lengthy legs he sought the foe,
    But not like yours, my spider.

French shepherds when their sheep they watch,
    On stilts prodigious ramble;
How sheepish look the flies you catch,
    When on your stilts you scramble!

The ostrich, which, in case of loss,
    In sand its eggs doth bury,
Runs not, I ween, with legs across,
    But in a plaguy hurry.

The catchpole, with a wretch in view,
    Runs at a pace enormous;
But what's their speed compared to you?
    You're lightening to a dormouse.

Contrasted thus, thy motions quick

> My corpulence determine;
> I can't endure this - where's my stick?
> And so take that, you vermin!

If the following poem be not one of the finest in the English language, and a glory to the literature of this country, "I'm a soused gurnet." I implore the judicious reader to mark the helter-skelter character of the versification, and the headlong precipitation with which the subject of this masterly poem is carried along. We feel ourselves borne onward with the author - we laugh, weep, grin, howl, shriek, yell, and sneeze, at the same time. But I will not detain the reader. Let him judge for himself.

ON FALLING DOWN STAIRS

A MYSTERY.

FIRST FLIGHT.

> *"Fallen, fallen, fallen, fallen."*
> Dryden

Fate sometimes entraps us:
Hilloa! What a lapsus!
Pinch with fiery hot nippers,

The villain most rascally,
Who made these vile slippers,
For tumbling most Pascally.
The stairs crush like bulrushes,
Downward my skull rushes,
And without any more pause,
I've committed my forepaws
To the slender lath'd banister; -
Oh! my poor canister!
Here I go, swift as lightning,
All oil cloth and whitening;
What a crush! Fit to start a wall -
There goes the party wall!
Here's a fall in the tallow trade -
Away goes the balustrade!
As I sink the storm rises,
Like the eve of a crisis.
Like patent wheels, I know,
Head over heels I go.
Like a cit from the Bow monde,
Or a rock from Ben Lomond,
Or that ship when they gave a launch,
Or a hundred-pow'r avalanche;
Or the falls (what a staggerer)
Or the brawling Niagara.
What a bellowing and sneezing!
My speed is increasing;
I am now whirl'd without end,
And I'm doomed, without any lie,
To roll on eternally.

FLIGHT SECOND

"The glow-worm shows the matting to be near."
Shakespeare

The lamp brightly burning
Shows the end of this churning;
The lamp in the passage
Shows the end of this crashage.
Pell mell - helter skelter!
I'm as hot as a smelter.
Gadzooks, what a summerset!
June is ice to my summer's heat.
What knee-cracks and ankling;
Oh! Doctor Franklin!
Thou were right, my old Bostonite:
I shall gather no moss to-night.
If one rolling stone, thrifty too,
Gather none, how should fifty-two?
But there's joy for my fat at last,
For I'm squat on the mat at last.
Send for the doctor,
The medicine concoctor;
Has he no recipes
For falls down a precipice!
Let him brush up his pharmacy -
Oil that would calm a sea,
Scarce will suffice to heal
All that's not nice to feel;
These bruises and tumours,
Worse than King Montezuma's
When (would he'd been less able!)

> Cortez drubbed the poor Mexicans,
> With such strength inexpressible,
> There's no word for't in Lexicons.
> To my mind every token stares,
> As I sit on the broken stairs,
> And recalls the precarious
> Fortune of Marius,
> Of whom, sitting at no rath age
> By the ruins of Carthage,
> I should be for a painting fit,
> But I'm off in a fainting fit.

With this sublime production I close my extracts for the present. I may, probably, upon a future occasion, indulge the reader with a few more selections from Mr. Lambert's papers, without prejudice to the two quarto volumes which Mr. Churton has consented to publish. I may, perhaps, present to the public, extracts from his Diary, - A treatise on Chivalry, written at a very early age, which he has facetiously called "Young's Knight Thoughts;" and a series of papers of a rather caustic nature, composed under the assumed name of Ralph Verjuice, which he has wittily been pleased to designate "R. V's Meditations." But of this more hereafter.

OMEGA.

MUSIC AND FRIENDS;

OR,

PLEASANT RECOLLECTIONS

OF

A Dilettante.

BY WILLIAM GARDINER.

IN TWO VOLUMES.

VOL. I.

LONDON:
LONGMAN, ORME, BROWN, AND LONGMAN.
COMBE AND CROSSLEY, LEICESTER.

MDCCCXXXVIII.

from
MUSIC AND FRIENDS:
Or, Pleasant Recollections of a Dilettante Vol. 1
By William Gardiner
Published 1838

Though our town could not vie with the Islington Hercules, we have produced the largest and heaviest man in the world. Daniel Lambert and myself were boys together, and as I lived next door to him, I watched his growth for several years. At the age of ten, he was a tall, strong lad, of a very quiet disposition, not at all inclining to be jolly, but possessing a fine open countenance. Soon after the age of fourteen he began to thicken rapidly; like Milo, with the calf, I have often carried him upon my back, but not when he became an ox. He was very fond of bathing, and his corpulency enabled him to perform extraordinary feats in the water. He was the envy of boys learning to swim, for while they were struggling to keep their heads above water, he would lie, like a whale, motionless upon the surface. During the summer months he was never so happy as when wallowing for hours in the river, rolling over and over like a hippopotamus; and as his weight increased, this desire increased also. The great use he made of this luxury probably relaxed the skin and tended to increase his bulk. Mr. Lambert was highly sensitive upon the subject of his huge appearance; and when he ventured out, was aware that it drew upon him the general gaze. With a cultivated mind, I might say above his station in life, he could not bear this exposure, and soon gave up his ordinary walks, remaining constantly at home. A life so sedentary operated to make him still more corpulent. In summer he could only enjoy the fresh air by sitting at his door, and that always without his coat. Dr. Hague, the university professor of music in Cambridge, having called upon me, I took him to see that Roman curiosity, the Jewry wall, near St. Nicholas' Church; and as we were going to view the room where King Richard the Third slept the night before the fight in Bosworth field, we had occasion to pass Mr. Lambert's house. He was sitting at the door, and the moment my friend caught a sight of him, in a fit of astonishment he made a full stop, and exclaimed "Mercy upon us, what a sight!" I walked on, knowing how much Mr. Lambert disliked the rude gaze of a stranger, and entered into conversation with him to take off the effect of Hague's astonishment; but Lambert followed the little doctor with his keen eye, and frowned upon him as he passed us, till he was out of sight. On rejoining the professor, I found him so filled with amazement that the sights I had in store for him claimed none of his attention compared with what he had unexpectedly seen. The quantity of cloth required to make his clothes was immense; and as he increased, I recollect he expressed to me the great difficulty he had in procuring stockings large enough. There was at that time a new invented stocking, called knotted hose, which was wrought lengthways upon the frame; I put him upon wearing these, as they could be made of any width. I think he measured forty inches round the calf. When he walked, there was a lightness in his step that was surprising; he had a voice clear and agreeable and sang with ease and taste. He was remarkably temperate, and frequently tried the experiment of abstinence, without any apparent diminution of bulk. When unrestrained, he would eat an entire leg of mutton.

Mr. Lambert was exceedingly fond of the sports of the field, and was curious in the breed of his dogs, and game fouls, which attracted to his house many country gentlemen. This was a delicate way of satisfying their curiosity, and by the sale of these animals something was contributed to his support. This source of revenue, however, began to decline, and his circumstances, at length, compelled him to form an alliance with a Mr. Pearson, much against his will; and he first submitted to be shown for a sight in Piccadilly, London. When I visited town, I called upon him as a friend, and soon discovered that he was distressed at my seeing him in a situation so degrading. He got up from his enormous chair (a thing he rarely did) and shook me by the hand. That his sensibility was wounded was evident during my stay, by the rebuff he gave a gentleman he thought too particular in his inquiries. He died, aged 36, at Stamford, on the 21st of June, 1809, and when last weighed he was 52 stones 11 lbs; but he had so increased since that time that his attendant told me he probably could not be less than 57 stones at the time of his decease.

A person quite as extraordinary for his diminutive size and weight was the Count Borwlaski, who resided with us for some time in Leicester. He was a neat, finished, little figure of a man, only 28 inches high. * I remember his coming in a sedan to one of our concerts at the town hall in full dress, wearing his Polish order, bag-wig, and sword. It was the custom then, and still is, with the Leicester people, to have a dance after the concert. The Count disencumbered himself of his sword and joined in the dance. He paid a visit to Mr. Lambert, who was very much diverted by the interview, looking down upon him, like an owl upon a tom-tit. Mr. Lambert asked what quantity of cloth the Count required for a coat, and how many he thought his would make him. "Not many," answered Borwlaski, "I take goot large piece cloth myself - almost tree quarters of yard." At this rate one of Mr. Lambert's sleeves would be abundantly sufficient for the purpose. The Count felt one of Mr. Lambert's legs; "Ah, mine Gott!" he exclaimed, "pure flesh and blood; I feel de warm; no deception! I am pleased; for I did hear it was deception." Mr. Lambert asked if his lady was alive, on which he replied, "No, she is dead, and (putting his finger significantly to his nose) I am not very sorry, for when I affronted her, she put me on the mantel-shelf for punishment."

* The Polish nobleman, Borwlaski, was well made, active, and intelligent; he measured 28 inches, and he had a brother of 34 inches, and a sister of 21. - *Curiosities of Medicine.*

Extract from
A GREAT IDEA
By Charles Dickens
HOUSEHOLD WORDS
Published 21st August 1852

For the stout man, who should represent the heavy father of my company, I would have somebody like Daniel Lambert. Lambert's name is known better than his history, and the lives of great men should not be forgotten. He was born at Leicester in 1770. His immediate ancestors in the paternal line had been a huntsman and a cock-fighter. His father became a prison-keeper, and retiring from office, was succeeded by the son. Daniel was then a strong young man, given to game sports, who since the age of nineteen, had promised to be heavy. A year after his appointment as a keeper in the prison the great increase in his size commenced, but he remained still active, was a good swimmer, and through the buoyancy of his fat could carry two men on his back across the river. In 1805, by new arrangements of the magistrates, Daniel's occupation in the prison went, and Daniel, though a young man, received a compensating pension of fifty pounds a year for life. He retired upon his other occupations in the breeding of game-cocks, terriers, and such matters as suited his hereditary taste; his bulk, however, had increased so much that he decided in 1806 to remove to London, where he took rooms in Piccadilly, and made a show of his body at the small charge of one shilling from each visitor. His rooms were well filled, many coming more than once to stare; a banker in the City boasted that he had indulged himself in a pound's worth of the edifying spectacle. When it was not the London season, Lambert made provincial tours, or rested at home among game-chickens and dogs, studying his one volume of literature, the Racing Calendar. He kept at one time thirty terriers, and his setters and pointers fetched prices at Tattersall's varying from twelve to forty-one guineas. Nine of his dogs were sold for two hundred and eighteen guineas.

Lambert was a cheerful and temperate man, a strict water-drinker. He was an exhibition only for three years. In 1809 he was found dead in his room one morning at Stamford, at which town he had arrived in apparent health the day before. On his arrival he had sent for the printer and entrusted to him a handbill announcing his appearance the next day before an enlightened public. He was buried in St. Martin's burial ground, and his virtues were carefully mustered on a monumental tablet in the following inscription: -

"In remembrance of that prodigy in nature Daniel Lambert, a native of Leicester, who was possessed of an excellent and convivial mind, and in personal greatness he had no competitor. He measured three feet one inch round the leg, nine feet four inches round the body and weighed fifty-two stone eleven pounds (fourteen pounds to the stone). He departed this life on the 21st June 1809, aged thirty-nine years. As a testimony of respect this stone was erected by his friends in Leicester."

Daniel Lambert was not a monster in tallness - five feet eleven only; but I will say nothing of giants and dwarfs. Only a well-known friend of Lambert's may be mentioned, Count Borulawski, who, it is said, expressed no grief at his wife's death, because when they had a domestic difference, she used to put him on the mantelpiece. I mention this circumstance, because it may suggest a little comic business for my projected entertainment.

Extract from
FAT PEOPLE
By Charles Dickens
ALL THE YEAR ROUND
Published 19th November 1864

Walk up, Daniel Lambert, king of fat men! In 1803, Lambert was keeper of the old county bridewell in Leicester. He had, at that time, an invincible repugnance to have his weight ascertained, being annoyed at the comments made upon him as a mountain of adipose substance; but some of his acquaintances, determined to settle the matter, contrived one day to have a vehicle in which he was riding drawn over a road weighing-machine. We have no record at hand of his weight at that time; but changes having been made in the prison arrangements at Leicester, Lambert consented to come to London to exhibit himself - no longer unwilling to have his bulk and weight talked about. In 1806, the following advertisement appeared: "Mr. Daniel Lambert, of Leicester, the heaviest man that ever lived. At the age of thirty-six years he weighs upwards of fifty stone (fourteen pounds to a stone), or eighty-seven stones four pounds London weight (i.e. butcher's weight of eight pounds to the stone), which is ninety-one pounds more than the great Mr. Bright weighed. Mr Lambert will see company at his house, Number Fifty-three Piccadilly, next Albany, nearly opposite St. James's Church, from eleven to five o'clock. Tickets of Admission, One Shilling each." He was one of the lions of London for a time. His exhibition-room (what a famous place Piccadilly has been for giants, dwarfs, lean people, and fat people!) was visited by the high-born as well as by the vulgar; and he appears to have been respected as well as looked at, for he was a kind and sensible man. He was always shocked at the idea of any personal indignity or insult being cast upon him on the ground of his bulk, by coarse-minded persons; and this known susceptibility was generally respected. Mr. Lambert was healthy in spite of his obesity. Some years earlier, when he was thrice the weight of an ordinary man, he could carry a weight of five hundred pounds. During the last fifteen years of his life, he drank nothing but water, and was usually cheerful and good humoured. His bulk increased year by year, until, shortly before his death, in 1809, he attained the unprecedented weight of seven hundred and thirty-nine pounds (nearly fifty-three stones). His coffin was seventy-six inches long by fifty-two wide and contained a hundred and twelve square feet of elm. The coffin was regularly built upon axles and wheels; and not only the window, but also the side of a room, had to be taken down, to afford a passage for the bulky mass. The wheeled coffin was drawn to St. Martin's churchyard, where a gradual descent was made to the grave by excavating the ground. We remember seeing, a few years ago, at a bootmaker's in the City, a pair of shoes, the counterpart of some which had been made for the mighty Daniel by a former owner of the shop; they were, as Thomas Hood said of a stage-coachman's great-coat,

Too broad to be conceived by any narrow mind.

www.markblasdale.com

OTHER SELECTED TITLES:

The Reckoning of Thaddeus Pike
About Bloody Time
Harrison's Patch
Rewrapped

ABOUT THE AUTHOR

Born, raised and educated in the rural heart of England, MARK BLASDALE is an internationally acclaimed author, seasoned traveller, lecturer, biographer and historian.

A self-diagnosed coffee-addict, hopeless list-writer and self-proclaimed 'Spirit of Christmas', Mark's passion for writing stems from childhood when he was introduced to the works of Charles Dickens by a family friend. Now a serious collector of antiquarian volumes himself, and with influences that include Washington Irving, Mark Twain, John Keats, O'Henry, Damon Runyon, Percival C Wren and Paul Gallico, it's little surprise that Mark is a passionate advocate of the Novella, Literary Sketch and Short Story.

His first book, Keeping Christmas, was published in 2014. Subsequent titles include All the Year Round (latterly titled A Day in the Life of Dickens), Six Hills: Spencer Bridge, Twelve Tales of Christmas, Christmas Miscellany, The Reckoning of Thaddeus Pike, Harrison's Patch and 2019's About Bloody Time, and Rewrapped.

Mark's interests, hobbies and influences, though too vast and varied to fully document here, include American history and politics, Victorian literature, rugby, hiking, ink & wash painting, cappuccino in all its wondrous forms, Mr Daniel Lambert, the history and traditions of Christmas, the philosophy of Mr Bob Ross, the teachings of American author/raconteur Shelby Foote, anything remotely connected to Charles Dickens, and the music of The Beach Boys.

Mark is married to the photographer, Alison Blasdale. They have two children and a cat named Pepsi.

www.markblasdale.com

Printed in Great Britain
by Amazon